U.S. ENVIRONMENTAL PROTECTION AGENCY
OFFICE OF INSPECTOR GENERAL

I0429210

Audit Briefing Report

EPA Action Needed to Ensure Drinking Water State Revolving Fund Projects Meet the American Recovery and Reinvestment Act Deadline of February 17, 2010

Report No. 10-R-0049

December 17, 2009

Report Contributors: Janet Kasper
                                             Matthew Simber
                                             Khadija Walker
                                             Lawrence Gunn
                                             Melinda Burks
                                             Nancy Dao

Abbreviations

ARRA	American Recovery and Reinvestment Act of 2009
DWSRF	Drinking Water State Revolving Fund
EPA	U.S. Environmental Protection Agency
HQ	Headquarters
OIG	Office of Inspector General
OMB	Office of Management and Budget
PBR	Project Benefits Reporting (EPA Drinking Water State Revolving Fund Program)
SRF	State Revolving Fund

Cover photo: Photos taken by EPA OIG at an ARRA DWSRF project in North Manchester, Indiana.

At a Glance

Catalyst for Improving the Environment

Why We Did This Review

We conducted this audit to determine how the U.S. Environmental Protection Agency (EPA) is ensuring compliance with American Recovery and Reinvestment Act of 2009 (ARRA) requirements. Specifically, we reviewed: (1) what impediments exist to having projects under contract or construction by February 17, 2010; and (2) what steps EPA has taken to ensure projects meet this deadline.

Background

ARRA provided EPA $2 billion for the National Drinking Water State Revolving Fund Program (DWSRF). The Act also required the EPA Administrator to reallocate any funds where the project is not under contract or construction by February 17, 2010.

For further information, contact our Office of Congressional, Public Affairs and Management at (202) 566-2391.

To view the full report, click on the following link:
www.epa.gov/oig/reports/2010/20091217-10-R-0049.pdf

EPA Action Needed to Ensure Drinking Water State Revolving Fund Projects Meet the American Recovery and Reinvestment Act Deadline of February 17, 2010

What We Found

Facing a myriad of challenges, EPA and the States used various approaches to mitigate the risk that projects may not meet the ARRA deadline. As of November 1, 2009, 257 projects, totaling $323.9 million, were under contract. This represented only 17 percent of the $1.9 billion in ARRA funds awarded for DWSRF projects. Challenges the States faced included delays in contracting at the local level, State and local budget cuts, and difficulty understanding and implementing new ARRA requirements. EPA efforts to assist States included guidance documents, offers of assistance in letters to Governors, State visits, phone calls with States, and monitoring information that States submitted.

As a result of our audit work, we made three observations about what EPA can do to improve its processes for ensuring that States comply with ARRA.

- EPA is not aware of projects that are not under contract nationwide. EPA DWSRF management did not monitor projects at the national level because it believed that regional-level monitoring was appropriate.

- EPA has not established procedures with an action plan and milestone dates to assist States with projects not under contract, because it believed that all States will meet the deadline. EPA has started to develop procedures for reallocating funds in case States do not meet the deadline.

- EPA's ARRA Risk Mitigation (Stewardship) Plan does not contain specific actions the Agency will take to identify States at risk of not meeting the deadline. EPA senior management intended the plan to provide the Agency's strategy to monitor and mitigate risk in ARRA implementation, but the DWSRF program did not rely upon the framework.

EPA must reallocate funding if projects are not under contract by February 17, 2010. This reallocation will delay the use of ARRA funding, which will in turn delay the creation of jobs and the jumpstarting of the economy.

What We Recommend

We recommend that EPA identify and monitor projects not under contract, establish a contingency action plan, complete its written procedures, and specify the actions it will take in its ARRA Risk Mitigation (Stewardship) Plan.

UNITED STATES ENVIRONMENTAL PROTECTION AGENCY
WASHINGTON, D.C. 20460

December 17, 2009

MEMORANDUM

SUBJECT: EPA Action Needed to Ensure Drinking Water State Revolving Fund
Projects Meet the American Recovery and Reinvestment Act
Deadline of February 17, 2010
Report No. 10-R-0049

FROM: Melissa M. Heist *Melissa M. Heist*
Assistant Inspector General for Audit

TO: Peter S. Silva, Assistant Administrator
Office of Water

This is our report on the subject audit conducted by the Office of Inspector General (OIG) of the
U.S. Environmental Protection Agency (EPA). This report contains findings that describe the
problems the OIG has identified and corrective actions the OIG recommends. This report
represents the opinion of the OIG and does not necessarily represent the final EPA position.
Final determination on matters in this report will be made by EPA managers in accordance with
established audit resolution procedures.

The estimated cost of this report – calculated by multiplying the project's staff days by the
applicable daily full cost billing rates in effect at the time – is $424,756.

Action Required

We request that you provide a written response to this report by January 8, 2010. You should
include a corrective action plan for addressing the recommendations, with milestone dates for
completing the actions. If you do not concur with the recommendations, please provide
alternative actions for addressing the findings in the report. We have no objections to the further
release of this report to the public. This report will be available at http://www.epa.gov/oig.

If you or your staff have any questions, please contact me at 202-566-0899 or
heist.melissa@epa.gov, or Janet Kasper at 312-886-3059 or kasper.janet@epa.gov.

cc: Craig Hooks, Assistant Administrator, Office of Administration and Resources Management

EPA Action Needed to Ensure Drinking Water State Revolving Fund Projects Meet the American Recovery and Reinvestment Act Deadline of February 17, 2010

Briefing Report

The American Recovery and Reinvestment Act of 2009 (ARRA)

- ARRA had five main purposes:

  - Preserve and create jobs and promote economic recovery;

  - Assist those most impacted by the recession;

  - Provide investments needed to increase economic efficiency by spurring technological advances in science and health;

  - Invest in transportation, environmental protection, and other infrastructure that will provide long-term economic benefits; and

  - Stabilize State and local government budgets, in order to minimize and avoid reductions in essential services and counterproductive State and local tax increases.

Background: DWSRF Program

- The National Drinking Water State Revolving Fund (DWSRF) Program was established in 1996 by the Safe Drinking Water Act. The Act authorized EPA to award grants to States which in turn provide low cost loans and other assistance to eligible public water systems.

- In Fiscal Year 2009, Congress appropriated $829 million for the DWSRF program. ARRA provided $2 billion in funds for DWSRF.

- As of November 1, 2009, EPA had awarded over $1.9 billion in DWSRF ARRA funds, of which $73.8 million was disbursed (under 4%).

3

New ARRA Requirements

- ARRA introduced new requirements to the SRF Program:

  - Davis Bacon: All laborers and mechanics employed on the funded projects must be paid at prevailing labor rates determined by the Secretary of Labor.

  - Buy American: Projects must use American iron, steel, and manufactured goods in the funded projects.

  - Green Project Reserve: States must use at least 20% of funds for projects to address green infrastructure, water or energy efficiency improvements, or other environmentally innovative activities.

  - Reporting: States and agencies must provide specific reports on use of ARRA funds.

  - Reallotment: The EPA Administrator will reallocate funds appropriated where projects are not under contract or construction by February 17, 2010 (12 months after the date of ARRA enactment).

Audit Objectives

- What impediments exist to having projects under contract or construction by February 17, 2010?

- What steps has EPA taken to ensure projects meet this deadline?

Scope and Methodology

- We conducted this performance audit from June to December 2009 in accordance with *Government Auditing Standards* issued by the Comptroller General of the United States. Those standards require that we plan and perform the audit to obtain sufficient, appropriate evidence to provide a reasonable basis for our findings and conclusions based on our audit objectives. We believe that the evidence obtained provides a reasonable basis for our findings and conclusions based on our audit objectives.

Scope and Methodology cont'd

- The EPA OIG Audit Team:

  - Focused on DWSRF because other OIG teams were focusing their reviews on Clean Water SRF projects.

  - Interviewed EPA Headquarters DWSRF staff to determine their internal controls over how they are monitoring States' progress, identifying challenges, and mitigating risks.

Scope and Methodology cont'd

- Interviewed EPA staff in Regions 3, 4, 5, 6, 9, and 10 to obtain information about their efforts to monitor and assist States in meeting the 12-month deadline.

- Interviewed States' DWSRF representatives in Arizona, Delaware, Michigan, North Carolina, New York, Oregon, and Wisconsin to determine project progress for meeting the 12-month deadline. These States were selected based on varying climates, geographic regions, and dollar amounts of ARRA funding. We discussed issues that have impacted the pace of projects, and assessed how States were monitoring this progress.

Scope and Methodology cont'd

- The EPA OIG Audit Team:

  - Reviewed ARRA and the Office of Management and Budget's (OMB's) ARRA Implementation Guidance;

  - Reviewed EPA ARRA Guidance, DWSRF ARRA Program Plan, and EPA ARRA Risk Mitigation (Stewardship) Plan;

  - Reviewed Fiscal Year 2009 and/or 2010 State Intended Use Plans and Project Priority Lists for ARRA Funding; and

  - Compared data from various EPA tracking systems including the Project Benefits Reporting (PBR) System, Integrated Financial Management System (IFMS), and Office of the Chief Financial Officer Reporting and Business Intelligence Tool (ORBIT).

State Discussion Topics

- The EPA OIG Audit Team developed a questionnaire as a basis for interviews with the seven States. The main topics included:

  - How many DWSRF ARRA projects were under contract and the dollars associated with those projects;

  - Whether States included language in their loan agreements on meeting the 12-month deadline;

  - Whether States had contingency plans in place for projects that were at risk for not meeting the deadline;

  - What else could EPA do to assist States in ensuring projects meet the deadline; and

  - What specific challenges did States face in meeting the deadline.

What We Found

Status of Project Progress

As of November 1, 2009:

- In the seven States we reviewed, 97 of 241 (40%) planned projects were under contract or construction.

- In the PBR system, 42 of these 97 projects were reported. The other 55 projects were not in the PBR system.

- In the PBR system, 257 projects totaling $323.9 million were under contract (44 States reporting). This is 17% of the $1.9 billion awarded.

State Challenges

- States initially needed clarification on ARRA's new requirements and subsequent EPA guidance.

- ARRA accelerated the base program process in getting projects under contract.

Process	Normal (est.)	Recovery Act (est.)
Appropriation to EPA Grant Award to States	1 year*	2 – 6 months*
Grant Award to Project Under Contract	1 - 2 years*	2 – 12 months**

Source: *Interviews with EPA staff, ** Recovery Act Requirement

State Impediments

- Contracting with local government is not a speedy process. For example:

  - Some had their own bidding and contracting procedures;
  - Some municipalities did not meet in summer months;
  - Ordinances/Resolutions might have been required; and
  - Referendums might have delayed/cancelled projects.

- States also faced resource challenges including budget cuts and furlough days for State employees.

- Some States also had to amend statutory authority to implement new ARRA requirements.

Potential Risk 1: Buy American Waiver Process

- EPA Buy American Waiver Process may pose a potential risk in getting projects under contract. EPA estimates that Buy American waivers will be approved two weeks after the final application is submitted by the community. We have observed a deviation from this timeframe where EPA approval took over a month. This indicates a potential risk in getting the projects under contract by February 17, 2010.

- According to the November 4, 2009, Congressional Testimony of EPA's Senior Accountable Official for ARRA Programs, to date, the Agency has issued 23 project-specific waivers, with more expected in the coming months.

Potential Risk 2: ARRA Data Collection and Reporting

- Two of the seven States we interviewed expressed concern about resources focused heavily on ARRA reporting (as required by section 1512 of the Act). States expressed that collecting the required reporting data was a strain on State resources. In one State's opinion, the reporting effort took focus away from ensuring projects were getting under contract.

Potential Risk 3: ARRA Noncompliance

- ARRA established timeframes for projects to be under contract or construction. This required local recipients to speed up their contracting processes. This time frame increases the risk of non-compliance with ARRA requirements, such as Buy American provisions.

Other Matters Not Related to the 12-Month Deadline

- Two EPA Regions and two of the States we interviewed stated that ARRA's emphasis on readiness to proceed or green projects took priority over the base program's emphasis on funding projects with the greatest public health needs.

EPA and State Efforts and Noteworthy Achievements to Facilitate Project Progress

EPA Efforts and Achievements: Headquarters (HQ)

EPA Senior Management conducted a number of activities to assist States in meeting the 12-month deadline. They included:

- EPA Administrator sent two letters to State governors expressing her commitment to assist and partner with States to achieve the goals of ARRA.

- EPA Office of Water and Office of Administration and Resources Management called State officials who appeared to be facing challenges in meeting the deadline.

- EPA's Senior Accountable Official for ARRA Programs met with Representatives from the National Governors Association to listen to their concerns about the challenges they faced in accomplishing ARRA goals.

- EPA's Senior Accountable Official for ARRA Programs sent emails to ARRA Leads in each State reminding States of the February 17, 2010, deadline and offering Agency assistance to the States.

EPA Efforts and Achievements: HQ cont'd

- Office of Water established a National Water Program Economic Recovery Management Team.

- Headquarters DWSRF program staff visited Regions and conducted conference calls with States.

- The DWSRF Program conducted webcasts for stakeholders on Buy American, Davis Bacon, Green Reserve, and 1512 Reporting.

- EPA established a Buy American waiver process for project-specific waivers.

- The DWSRF Program issued guidance on ARRA requirements.

- The DWSRF Program established the PBR System to track project level data.

- The DWSRF Program conducted State analysis of financial drawdown and project progress data starting in October 2009, and weekly thereafter.

EPA Efforts and Achievements: Regions

- EPA Regions talked with States weekly or bi-weekly in the six Regions we interviewed.

- EPA Region 6 reported State project progress to the Regional Administrator on a weekly basis.

- EPA Region 4 Regional Administrator held conference calls with State Commissioners.

- EPA Regions 5 and 6 tracked State progress and updated information daily or weekly as projects came under contract.

EPA Efforts and Achievements: Regions cont'd

- EPA Region 5 conducted a regular analysis of States' draw downs of ARRA funds and compared the amounts to progress reported in PBR.

- Regions conducted joint training with the OIG to sub-recipients, contractors, and vendors on ARRA requirements and prevention of fraud, waste, and abuse.

- Regional staff, in conjunction with an EPA contractor, are conducting on-site reviews of some DWSRF ARRA and base program projects (August 2009 – January 2010).

State Efforts and Achievements

- Five States included language in their loan agreements/binding commitments with sub-recipients about meeting the February 17, 2010, deadline.

- All seven States established contingency dates or interim milestones prior to February 17, 2010, to assess project progress and potentially move funds to another project if projects are not ready to proceed to contract by the deadline.

State Efforts and Achievements cont'd

- The State of Arizona established a more stringent deadline of requiring projects to be under construction by February 17, 2010, not just under contract.

- The States of Arizona, Oregon, and New York planned to switch out funding from ARRA to base program if projects were identified as not ready to proceed to contract by the deadline.

Chart of State Contingency Dates and Actions

State	Contingency Date	Action
AZ	Jan 1, 2010	Contracts signed and submitted to State. On January 2, 2010, State will terminate loan contracts with construction start dates beyond February 17, 2010.
DE	Jan 1, 2010	Contracts signed. If not, State will move ARRA funding to other projects ready to proceed and substitute base funding.
MI	Jan 22, 2010	Loans must be signed. Notices to Proceed by February 17, 2010. If not, State will move funds to other projects already under contract.
NC	Oct 1, 2009	Contracts signed. If not, State might move ARRA funds to other eligible projects ready to proceed.

State Contingency Dates cont'd

State	Contingency Date	Action
NY	Jan 1, 2010	Contracts signed. If not, State will move ARRA funds to other projects and substitute base funding.
OR	Feb 16, 2010	Contracts signed. If not, State will move ARRA funds to other projects and substitute base funding.
WI	Oct 1, 2009	Contracts signed. If not, State planned to move ARRA funds to other eligible projects on the funding list. Remaining funds will be used to increase principal forgiveness of projects already under contracts.

Conclusion

- States are facing a myriad of challenges: local government contracting, resource issues, and understanding and implementing ARRA requirements.

- EPA and States have used varying approaches to mitigate the risks for projects not being able to meet the ARRA deadline.

Observations and Recommendations

ARRA Requirements

ARRA states that:

" … the Administrator shall reallocate funds appropriated herein for the Clean and Drinking Water State Revolving Funds (Revolving Funds) where projects are not under contract or construction within 12 months of the date of enactment of this Act … "

EPA Guidance

- EPA's SRF ARRA Guidance states:

  "The Administrator must reallocate any funds that do not meet the required deadline for contracts or construction. In order to implement this provision, EPA will deobligate funds from awarded grants that have not been committed to projects and that are not under contract or construction by February 17, 2010."

Observation 1

- EPA ARRA Guidance and grant agreements require States to use the PBR system to track project-level data on a weekly basis. States are required to report loan agreements executed and first and last construction contracts signed for the project.

- Government Accountability Office Internal Control Standards state that information should be recorded and communicated to management to determine whether the organization is meeting its goals.

Observation 1 cont'd

- EPA is not aware of projects not under contract on a national level. The PBR system only captures project-specific information once the State has executed a loan agreement with local borrowers. It does not capture projects not under contract, or projects under contract that do not have a loan agreement executed.

- Not all the Regions are collecting information from States about projects not under contract. The Agency does not know whether States will have all projects in compliance with the February 17, 2010, deadline. For example:

  - Regions lacked a consistent approach in monitoring States' progress toward meeting the February 17, 2010, deadline. One Region is monitoring projects not under contract, while another Region is monitoring States by comparing PBR data to State financial draws, as required by EPA ARRA Monitoring Guidance.

Observation 1 (cont'd)

- EPA DWSRF management believes that project-level monitoring is appropriately carried out at the regional rather than the national level and expects Regions' approaches to vary according to the specific needs and circumstances that Regions encounter in working with States. EPA DWSRF management noted that no State intends to face reallotment.

- EPA cannot be informed about State progress if they don't collect critical information from States to determine if projects will be under contract or construction by the February 17, 2010 deadline.

34

Observation 2

- OMB Circular A-123 states that internal controls are an integral component of an organization's management that provides reasonable assurance that the Agency complies with laws and regulations. February, 17, 2010, is a key compliance deadline and internal controls have not been fully established to provide a reasonable assurance this deadline will be met.

- EPA discussed reallotment in March 2009 guidance to recipients, and is developing more detailed procedures on the reallotment process.

Observation 2 cont'd

- EPA has communicated the importance of meeting February 17, 2010, to States. However, EPA has not established procedures with an action plan and milestone dates, to assist States that have a large number of proposed projects not under contract prior to the deadline because it believes all States will meet the deadline. This belief contrasts sharply with the reality that only 17 percent of the funds were under contract as of November 1, 2009, 3 ½ months before the ARRA deadline.

- Without developing and implementing an action plan, EPA cannot provide a reasonable assurance that the ARRA compliance deadline will be met.

Observation 3

- OMB's ARRA Implementation Guidance Section 3.12 states:

    "...agencies should develop mitigation plans that align with specific risks. At a minimum, agencies should prepare mitigation plans for those risks with the highest probability of occurrence and the greatest impact if not mitigated. Whenever possible, agencies should identify quantifiable measures of performance, including ranges of acceptable and unacceptable performance. Along with mitigation actions, agencies should also identify a "trigger" to determine if it should initiate a contingency plan. Triggers could include program performance falling outside of an acceptable range or not completing critical actions by specific dates."

Observation 3 cont'd

- On July 8, 2009, the Acting Chief Financial Officer, in announcing the Stewardship Plan, stated: "The Stewardship Plan lays out the Agency's strategy to monitor and mitigate risk in the implementation of the Recovery Act."

Observation 3 cont'd

- EPA's ARRA Risk Mitigation (Stewardship) Plan does not contain specific actions be taken to identify States at risk for not meeting the February 17, 2010, deadline.

- Example 1: EPA does not collect the information to identify at-risk projects. The Plan requires monitoring activities to identify points at which EPA would be alerted to a problem. EPA planned to collect monitoring information from the PBR system, site visits, and phone calls to States. However, the EPA March 2 ARRA guidance only requires States to put data into PBR when a loan agreement is executed. PBR does not capture information on those projects without an executed loan agreement. Therefore, EPA does not have the information it needs to identify State projects at risk for not having contracts signed by February 17, 2010.

Observation 3 cont'd

- Example 2: EPA does not identify a responsible official or an action to be taken in response to an identified risk. The Plan does not specify the points at which additional action will be taken once a risk is identified. The Plan also does not assign the EPA official responsible for ensuring additional mitigation actions are taken when needed.

Observation 3 cont'd

- <u>Example 3:</u> <u>Agency does not describe contingency plans.</u> The Plan does not describe the actions the Agency will take when monitoring and control activities indicate that there is an increased risk that goals are not met prior to the February 17, 2010, deadline.

- EPA DWSRF management stated its actions to ensure projects are under construction by the deadline has not been restricted to the framework of the ARRA stewardship plan. While the DWSRF is taking action to address the risk of noncompliance with the law, the stewardship plan is not fully serving as the framework EPA senior management intended it to be.

Possible Outcomes

- States will be subject to Agency reallotment of funds if projects are not under contract by February 17, 2010.

- Reallotment will delay the use of ARRA funding and therefore the impact of creating jobs and jumpstarting the economy.

- Section 1603 of ARRA stipulates the Agency will lose funding if funds are not obligated by September 30, 2010.

Recommendations

Recommendation 1

The Assistant Administrator for the Office of Water should establish a nationwide and consistent process to identify and monitor the progress of DWSRF projects prior to February 17, 2010, that are not under contract or construction.

Recommendation 2.1

The Assistant Administrator for the Office of Water should establish and implement an action plan, with milestone dates, by which it will request contingency actions from States prior to February 17, 2010, for those projects identified as not being under contract or construction.

Recommendation 2.2

The Assistant Administrator for the Office of Water should complete its written procedures for reallocating the funds for States that do not meet the deadline.

Recommendation 3

The Assistant Administrator for the Office of Water should specify the actions it will take to address the risk that projects will not meet the February 17, 2010, deadline in EPA's ARRA Risk Mitigation (Stewardship) Plan.

Status of Recommendations and Potential Monetary Benefits

		RECOMMENDATIONS				POTENTIAL MONETARY BENEFITS (in $000s)	
Rec. No.	Page No.	Subject	Status[1]	Action Official	Planned Completion Date	Claimed Amount	Agreed To Amount
1	44	Establish a nationwide and consistent process to identify and monitor the progress of DWSRF projects prior to February 17, 2010, that are not under contract or construction.		Assistant Administrator, Office of Water			
2.1	45	Establish an action plan with milestone dates, by which it will request contingency actions from States prior to February 17, 2010, for those projects identified as not being under contract or construction.		Assistant Administrator, Office of Water			
2.2	46	Complete its written procedures for reallocating the funds for States that do not meet the deadline.		Assistant Administrator, Office of Water			
3	47	Specify the actions it will take to address the risk that projects will not meet the February 17, 2010, deadline in EPA's ARRA Risk Mitigation (Stewardship) Plan.		Assistant Administrator, Office of Water			

[1] O = recommendation is open with agreed-to corrective actions pending
C = recommendation is closed with all agreed-to actions completed
U = recommendation is undecided with resolution efforts in progress

Distribution

Office of the Administrator
Assistant Administrator, Office of Water
Assistant Administrator, Office of Administration and Resources Management
Regional Administrators, Regions 1-10
Agency Follow-up Official (the CFO)
Agency Follow-up Coordinator
Principal Deputy Assistant Administrator, Office of Administration and Resources Management
Deputy Assistant Administrator, Office of Water
Director, Office of Ground Water and Drinking Water, Office of Water
Deputy Director, Office of Ground Water and Drinking Water, Office of Water
General Counsel
Associate Administrator for Congressional and Intergovernmental Relations
Associate Administrator for Public Affairs
Audit Follow-up Coordinator, Office of Water
Audit Follow-up Coordinator, Office of Administration and Resources Management
Audit Follow-up Coordinators, Regions 1-10
Acting Inspector General